GARTH ENNIS
WRITER

STEVE DILLON
ARTIST

MATT HOLLINGSWORTH
COLORIST

CLEM ROBINS
LETTERER

GLENN FABRY
COVERS

PREACHER CREATED BY GARTH ENNIS AND STEVE DILLON

PREACHER: GONE TO TEXAS. Published by DC Comics. Cover, introduction and compilation copyright © 1996 DC Comics. All Rights Reserved.
Originally published in single magazine form as PREACHER 1-7. Copyright © 1995 Garth Ennis and Steve Dillon. All Rights Reserved.
All characters, their distinctive likenesses and related indicia featured in this publication are trademarks of Garth Ennis and Steve Dillon.
Vertigo is a trademark of DC Comics. The stories, characters, and incidents featured in this publication are entirely fictional.
DC Comics does not read or accept unsolicited submissions of ideas, stories, or artwork.

DC Comics, 1700 Broadway, New York, NY 10019
A Warner Bros. Entertainment Company
Printed in Canada. Seventh Printing.
ISBN: 1-56389-261-8
Cover painting by Glenn Fabry.
Publication design by Eddie Ortiz.

FOREWORD

by Joe R. Lansdale

First off, as for PREACHER, well, there ain't two just like it. We'll make that a little more immediate like. We'll even repeat it for the drowsy. THERE AIN'T TWO JUST LIKE IT.

It's kinda part Western, part Crime story, part Horror story, and partly just fucked-up strange. Well, a lot fucked-up strange.

It's a universe within itself. An alternate universe. As a Texan, I find all the Texas business more than a little interesting, even if the dialogue and turns of phrase are now and then off, and more British than Texian. Garth struggles now and then to be too Texan. But the spirit is right — or at least the mythical spirit is. Texas is, after all, a state of mind as well as an actual terrain. It is anything and everything you want it to be, and none of these. It is the Mount Olympus of hard-boiled stories with Western grit. It might be nice if now and then folks noticed that good people and good events come from Texas as well as the bad. but the myth of this rebel universe prevails, and if it must prevail, it's nice to know that there are writers like Garth Ennis playing with that myth in a smart and savvy way.

Got to tell you, stories like this, people read them and say, "This is a hoot." A way to wind down from the more serious stuff. They see the raw language and the action and the brutality, the splatter, and they see little else. Most of the time they are right. But PREACHER...

Let me clue you. This is just as serious as any of Vertigo's highly-praised "intellectual" stuff, and better than a lot of it. Don't confuse "intelligent" with "intellectual." Pretention can confuse a soul if they're not paying attention. This stuff, well, pretentious it ain't, but smart it is.

And it's fun. Well, is "fun" the word I'm looking for here? Maybe, maybe not. Fascinating. That's the word.

And we all know it's a comic book. That it isn't real. It's our chance to look at the dark side without having to be a part of it. It's like watching an alligator eat a pig. Ugly, but still mesmerizing. Especially since we're not the pig. I wonder what the pig's point of view is, looking up from its unique position to see curious faces looking down on its last moments. But that's another consideration.

Another thing about PREACHER, and I'm damn sure not giving anyone who has read it a news flash: It's scary as a psychopathic greased gerbil with a miner's hat and a flashlight and your bare asshole in sight. Actually, it's scarier than that. This stuff really bothered me, and at times I thought it might be a little too much. But I found myself waiting for the next issue with anticipation. I can't say that about most comics. In fact, I start a lot of comics that I don't finish, and considering it takes so little time to read a comic, I guess that's a serious statement of some kind.

This stuff is unique. It's intriguing. It touches on a base level. Makes things crawl around in the viscera (Where is that gerbil with the flashlight anyway?) and the brain. It stays true to its intent as well. It doesn't suddenly go from being this dark and terrible tale to being warm and squishy with a catch in its throat. You get yourself a rattlesnake, it'll bite today, and it'll bite tomorrow. And unless it's toothless, it'll bite two years from now. A rattlesnake is always a rattlesnake, and Garth's tale is always just what it started out to be—grim and grey with flashes of blackness.

And while we're praising the writing, the mood, let's talk about the artwork, which ain't slouchy either. It puts the paint on the conception, brightens it up and makes it burn. Or maybe, in this case, darkens it up and makes it smolder. Steve Dillon's art is perfect for the story. It puts tainted saliva on the fangs of Garth Ennis's prose. It puts the shadow behind the curtain and makes the blood on the floor crawl.

These first seven comics, collected here together, are to my way of thinking a milestone for Vertigo. This is unique stuff, a hole in the dike of sameness. And the water rushing through that hole, spider-webbing the concrete of the dam, cracking it, blasting it apart, is a nasty black water leaking directly from the brains of Messrs. Ennis and Dillon. This is not to imply that Garth Ennis or Steve Dillon are bad folks. I don't know them. But I will say this: They know fucked-up when they see it, and like Flannery O'Connor, they're willing to put their fingers on it and make it squirm for your observation.

I'm not sure it's a learning experience, but it's a thinking experience, and most important, as I said early on, it's unique, and I hope its uniqueness does not encourage a hundred writers to go out and try to repeat it. What they will come up with is just meanness for meanness' sake. It won't have the edge, the special feel of PREACHER. They'll just be imitations. Because there is only one Garth Ennis, and only one Steve Dillon, and only one PREACHER, a tale out of Ireland, dragged through Texas with a bloody hard-on, wrapped in barbed wire and rose thorns. And it's out to get you.

Joe R. Lansdale

Nacogdoches, Texas

...AND THE LESSON'S BEGUN.♪

THE TIME OF THE PREACHER

GARTH ENNIS
WRITER

STEVE DILLON
ARTIST

MATT HOLLINGSWORTH - COLORIST

CLEM ROBINS - LETTERER

JULIE ROTTENBERG - ASS'T EDITOR

STUART MOORE - EDITOR

PREACHER CREATED BY

GARTH ENNIS and STEVE DILLON

REASON EVERYONE IN ANNVILLE WAS IN CHURCH LAST SUNDAY WAS BECAUSE OF WHAT HAPPENED ON SATURDAY NIGHT.

SEE, I'D BEEN HAVING KIND OF A CRISIS OF FAITH, AND I'D STAYED UP LATE TO TALK IT THROUGH WITH MY GOOD BUDDY JACK...

UH... REVER'ND CUSTER?

JESSE'LL DO JUST FINE, LEONARD.

JESSE... SURE. JUST WE DON'T SEE TOO MUCH OF YOU IN HERE, IS ALL.

BEEN MEANING TO FIX THAT. HOW 'BOUT A BEER?

...COMIN' UP.

ALL RIGHT IF I SIT HERE?

SURE.

AAHHHH.

THAT'S GOOD BEER, LEONARD.

HELL, YOU CAN ALMOST TASTE IT THROUGH THE GODDAMN WATER.

I--I--REVER'ND, I DUNNO WHAT YOU--

AW, C'MON LENNY, WHOLE *TOWN* KNOWS YOU DO IT! MAKES THE HORSEPISS LASTS THAT LITTLE BIT LONGER, RIGHT?

GODDAMMIT, REVER'ND--!

TOWN THIS SMALL HASN'T TOO MANY SECRETS, AM I RIGHT? AN' YOU KNOW THE FUNNY THING? YOU KNOW WHO GETS TO HEAR 'EM ALL?

ME.

GOOD OL' REVEREND CUSTER, SITTIN' IN HIS CHURCH TO BE LAUGHED AT ON SUNDAYS--I OVERHEAR IT, OR SOMEONE TELLS ME *IN THE STRICTEST CONFIDENCE*, OR I JUST READ THE PAPER AN' PUT TWO AN' TWO TOGETHER...

STUFF EVERYONE KNOWS AN' THINKS NOBODY KNOWS, LEAST OF ALL YOUR DUMB-ASS SONUVABITCH *PREACHER*.

MARK! MARK BANNON! ATE DOGSHIT FOR A DARE OUTSIDE THIS VERY ESTABLISHMENT!

FUH--FUH--FUCK YOU...!

WHERE'S HARVEY?

COULD FEED HALF OF RWANDA ON THE GRANTS YOU GET FOR THAT FARM, HARVE...

ALL ABOVE BOARD, REVEREND.

YOU BETCHA.

15

LIKE THE MOVIE KATE SHOT IN YOUR BARN, HUH? JUST HER AN' A PIEBALD STALLION-- WENT STRAIGHT TO VIDEO, WAY I HEAR IT.

I'VE NEVER SEEN THIS WOMAN BEFORE IN MY LIFE--

uh--

BUT LEAVIN' ASIDE MICHAEL HERE--WHO'S GOTTA BE THE ONLY MAN FROM ANNVILLE THAT EVER WENT TO CALIFORNIA --LET'S MEET THE STARS OF THE SHOW...

REVER'ND, YOU'VE HAD A LITTLE TOO MUCH TO--REVER'ND--

PAT AN' TERRY MORROW.

NOW YOU BETTER JUST WATCH YOUR FUCKIN' MOUTH, CUSTER...

WHO RAPED THAT HITCHER GIRL NO MATTER WHAT THEIR DADDY PAID JUDGE SHEBIN.

I SEE YOU EVERY SUNDAY, THE FEW OF YOU BOTHER TO SHOW UP, AN' YOU THINK YOU CAN SING A FEW GOD-DAMN HYMNS AN' THEN ACT LIKE SAVAGES FOR THE REST OF THE WEEK?

OR HOW MANY TIMES THIS TOWN CAN CHANGE THE GODDAMN SUBJECT.

YOU'RE FUCKIN' DRIVIN' ME INSANE AN' I'M HERE TO TELL YOU, THAT AIN'T THE WAY IT WORKS--

WUHH!!

THIS USED TO BE MY BROTHER. AN HOUR AGO WE WERE CIRCLING IN THE STRATOSPHERE WHEN YOUR *ENTITY* CAME CHARGING OUT OF THE RISING SUN AND DID THIS TO HIM.

WHAT ARE YOU GOING TO DO ABOUT IT?

YOU'RE SAYING *GENESIS* DID THIS?

YES. THE CROSSBRED *WHELP* YOU ADEPHI FOPS ARE MEANT TO BE LOOKING AFTER. A COMET WITH THE FACE OF AN INFANT.

GENESIS.

YOU CAN'T BE SURE--

CAN'T BE SURE *NOTHING.* YOU BUNCH OF SYCOPHANTS HAD BETTER GET GENESIS BACK BEFORE IT CAUSES ANY TROUBLE DOWN ON EARTH. START *NOW.*

AND JUST YOU REMEMBER WHO'S IN CHARGE AROUND HERE.

THEY WERE ONLY LEFT IN CHARGE ...

AND THAT'S ALL THE AUTHORITY THEY NEED.

THE THING TO DO IS TREAT THE SERAPHI WITH KID GLOVES--

THE THING TO DO IS GET GENESIS BACK, POST BLOODY HASTE. YOU STUDIED IT--WHAT DOES IT WANT ON EARTH?

A SOUL.

COME AGAIN?

MY EXAMINATIONS REVEALED THAT GENESIS WAS DEVELOPING AN IDENTIFICATION WITH HUMAN CONCERNS, EVEN THE BEGINNINGS OF A MORALITY, WHICH WOULD HAVE COME FROM BOTH THE PARENTS.

IT WILL ATTEMPT TO BOND WITH A FULLY DEVELOPED CONSCIOUSNESS.

WITH A SOUL.

WE CAN'T LET THAT HAPPEN.

IF *THAT THING* ACHIEVES FULL SENTIENCE, THE GAME IS WELL AND TRULY UP FOR ALL OF US. WE NEED SOMEONE TO GO AFTER IT...

SOMEONE WHO NEVER FAILS--

AND... NEVER STOPS...

WAIT A *MINUTE*--!

PILO?

MM?

YOU CAN'T--

I'VE GOT TO, FIORE.

I'VE GOT A JOB FOR YOU, MY FRIEND.

ANYTHING, DEBLANC! YOU KNOW YOU ONLY HAVE TO ASK!

GO TO BOOT HILL AND WAKE THE SAINT OF KILLERS.

ME?

SO I WOKE UP OUTSIDE THE CHURCH IN A POOL OF PUKE, ROUND ABOUT SIX A.M. NOW, THE SERVICE USUALLY STARTED AT NINE--

WHOA-WHOA-WHOA, HOLD' ON...

WE'LL LEAVE YOU IN YOUR POOL OF PUKE FOR THE MINUTE. THIS IS WHERE ME AN' TULIP COME IN.

SO WHAT? THAT'S GOT NOTHING TO DO WITH JESSE AND--

WELL, YOU WERE THE ONE WANTED TO GET IT ALL STRAIGHT IN OUR HEADS...

YOU DON'T HAVE TO...

IT'S OKAY.

GREAT! WELL, I WAS JUST ON MY WAY OUT OF DALLAS--I FANCIED A CHANGE OF DIET MORE THAN ANYTHING ELSE...

I BET YOU DID.

I'D TIMED IT TO PERFECTION--WHICH, AS YOU KNOW, JESSE, ISN'T LIKE ME AT ALL --AND HE SHOWED UP JUST LIKE THEY TOLD ME HE WOULD...

WERE YOU SCARED?

HELL NO.

BAR

OH, SHIT...

FUCK!

WELL DON'T JUST FUCKIN' SIT THERE! GET HER!

HHHH... MM.

YOU THINK THAT WAS SUPPOSED TO BE A HIT?

AW JESUS...! I GOTTA GET *OUTTA* HERE--

HA HA HA! AYE, WHAT THE FUCK. GET IN.

FUCKIN' *WHORE!*

GO!

MMF.

I REALLY APPRECIATE THIS--

DON'T MENTION IT. YOU'VE BRIGHTENED UP AN OTHERWISE BORING EVENING, LUV.

TULIP.

CASSIDY.

...EVERYONE IN ANNVILLE CAME TO CHURCH THE NEXT MORNING. *EVERYONE.* I USUALLY GOT MAYBE TWENTY PEOPLE SHOWING UP: THIS TIME I HAD DAMN NEAR TWO HUNDRED.

NOW, EITHER MY PRAYERS HAD BEEN ANSWERED AND THE WHOLE TOWN HAD SEEN THE LIGHT AT ONCE--

OR THEY'D ALL HEARD ABOUT YOU GOIN' *MENTAL* THE NIGHT BEFORE.

"REVER'ND CUSTER'S LOSIN' HIS *MIND!* LET'S GO SEE; MAYBE HE'LL JERK OFF ON THE BIBLE OR SOMETHIN'!"

I FIGURED THAT WAS A LITTLE MORE LIKELY, BUT YOU ALWAYS HOPE...

ONE LOOK AT THEIR FACES, AND I COULD TELL THE GOOD LORD WAS USING MY PRAYERS TO WIPE HIS ASS.

*uh...*GOOD MORNING.

IT--

IT SURE IS NICE TO SEE SO MANY OF YOU FOLKS HERE THIS MORNING...

JUST OUT OF INTEREST--WHAT WOULD YOUR *SERMON* HAVE BEEN ABOUT?

FORGIVENESS.

ANYWAY, THEN WHAT *HAPPENED* WAS--

MY GOD...!

CASSIDY HAD PULLED OVER JUST BEFORE DAWN. THEN HE GOT IN THE BACK, COVERED HIMSELF IN A TARPAULIN, AND MADE ME *SWEAR* NOT TO TAKE IT OFF OF HIM.

THAT'S WHERE WE WERE WHEN I SAW THE FIRE...

HOLD ON. HIM DOING THIS DIDN'T MAKE YOU SUSPICIOUS?

OH, SO THE SECOND I SAW HIM SLEEPING LIKE THAT I SHOULD'VE FIGURED OUT WHAT HE IS? IT'S NOT EXACTLY A NORMAL--

RIGHT, *RIGHT*...

HEY! HEY!

THERE'S A *MUSHROOM CLOUD* DOWN THE ROAD--

I DON'T GIVE A FUCK! STOP!

YOU DIDN'T SAY NOT TO DRIVE THE TRUCK. ALL YOU SAID--

I THOUGHT IT WAS A BIT BLEEDIN' OBVIOUS!

I'M TELLIN' YOU, TULIP, *RIGHT FRIGGIN' NOW*: YOU PULL OVER AN' STOP THIS TRUCK OR ELSE!

I NOTICE YOU HAVEN'T STOPPED.

WELCOME TO ANNVILLE
PLEASE DRIVE CAREFULLY

35

THIS IS FUCKIN' CHARMIN', THIS IS.

NOT ONLY DO I PULL YOU OUT OF A FRIGGIN' FIREFIGHT, I THEN GIVE YOU A LIFT HALFWAY ACROSS TEXAS *NO QUESTIONS ASKED* --AN' THIS IS WHAT I GET FOR MY TROUBLE?

WELL, SEE AS SOON AS THE SUN GOES DOWN? YOU AN' I ARE GOIN' OUR SEPARATE WAYS, WEE GIRL...

IT'S LIKE A *BOMB* HIT IT...

IF IT'S AS BAD AS IT SOUNDS, WELL, FUCK KNOWS WHAT'S BEEN GOIN' ON AROUND HERE. YOU MIGHT WANT TO TAKE YOUR GUN.

NOT THAT I CARE WHAT HAPPENS TO YOU ONE WAY OR THE OTHER, LIKE.

TULIP.

36

JESUS, I'M DYIN' FOR A FAG. OR A CIGARETTE, I SHOULD SAY TO AVOID ANY TRANSATLANTIC CONFUSION. HOUL' ON 'TIL--

NO--

NO, THEIR MACHINE'S EMPTY. I'LL GO FIND A STORE OR SOMETHING. MARLBORO?

CAMELS.

WELL, PILGRIM...

COULDN'T HELP BUT NOTICE YA AIN'T MENTIONED ME YET.

38

MEEKER SAYS CARLINGTON'S SENDIN' A CHOPPER AN' A MARKSMAN, AN' EVERY MAN THEY GOT TO SPARE. HE WANTS YOU TO TALK TO SOME MEDIA PEOPLE--

YOU TELL HIM FUCK YOU.

TELL HIM HUGO ROOT SAYS FUCK YOU. TELL HIM I SEE ONE OF THEM MEDIA FUCKS, I'M GONNA HAUL 'EM DOWN TO DEERFORTH AN' SHOVE 'EM UP HIS FAGGOT ASS.

YOU CALLED THE F.B.I. IN ON THIS, SHERIFF?

YOU KNOW IT. PROCEEDURE.

YOU DON'T FIGURE, WAY THESE PEOPLE BEEN BLASTED TO GODDAMN BONES, WE SHOULD MAYBE WAIT FOR THE FEDS BEFORE WE COVER THE COUNTRY IN GUNS?

GOIN' WEAK SISTER ON ME, KENNY?

ALL I'M SAYIN' IS, COULD BE MORE THAN WE CAN HANDLE HERE--

COULD BE I'M GONNA SHIT ME THE KEYS TO GRACELAND TOMORROW, BUT I KINDA DOUBT THAT AS WELL. MARTIAN NIGGERS, KENNY.

P-TT

YOU WAIT AN' SEE.

40

TOLD YOU! HIS FUCKIN' HEAD'S CUT!

HE ALWAYS USED TO BE KIND OF, WELL, ECLECTIC--

BOLLICKS! ALL YOU HAVE TO DO TO BE ECLECTIC IN THIS COUNTRY IS OWN A CHILI PEPPERS ALBUM. WHAT *HE* IS, IS OFF HIS FUCKIN' ROCKER...

DO YOU MEAN LIKE WHEN YOU WERE CURIOUS ENOUGH TO DRIVE MY TRUCK INTO A SODDIN' DEATHZONE?

FOR JESUS' SAKE, TULIP, THIS BLOKE'S RIGHT AT THE EYE OF A FORCE TEN SHIT-STORM! CURIOSITY WON'T JUST *KILL* THE CAT, IT'LL BITE ITS HEAD OFF AND STUMP-FUCK THE REMAINS 'TIL THE SUN COMES UP!

NO, I'M CURIOUS ABOUT THIS--

WELL, I'M NOT HANGIN' AROUND HERE TO BE--HERE, HOLD' ON...I CAN SMELL COPS...

MM? WHAT D'YOU MEAN

YOU USELESS, PECKERWOOD, COCK-SUCKIN'--

SHERIFF ROOT?

SHERIFF ROOT...

...JUST WHEN THERE'S THE FIRST GODDAMN GLIMMER OF LIGHT, IT ALL HAS TO TURN TO SHIT...

WELL...

LOOKS LIKE THIS IS ASSHOLE NIGHT. *ARMED* ASSHOLE NIGHT.

FIGURE YOU GOT YOURSELF SOME GUNS IN THEM BELTS, BOY.

YEAH.

BUT YOU DON'T LOOK TO ME LIKE THE MAN WHO'LL TAKE 'EM.

BANG.

NEXT: JUST A FEW COPS

RIGHT AFTER HE SAYS I AIN'T TAKIN' HIS GUNS, HE SHIFTS HIS COAT BACK AN' SURE ENOUGH HE'S WEARIN' PISTOLS IN CROSSED GUNBELTS.

ALL *OUR* GUNS ARE STILL ON THE GROUND--

RIGHT, THIS IS FROM WHEN YOUR FIRST SUSPECT TOLD YOU AND YOUR OFFICERS TO DROP 'EM. AND YOU COULDN'T HELP YOURSELVES.

P-T--

LIKE I SAID.

SHERIFF ROOT, HOLD OFF--*LOOK* AT HIM--

ALL'VE YOU PICK YOUR GUNS UP.

SHERIFF--

THEN THERE'S THIS BLUR AN' THE FUCKER'S SHOOTIN'.

SO HE DREW ON YOU.

AIN'T WHAT I SAID. A BLUR AN' THEN SHOOTIN'.

I DIDN'T SEE NO DRAW.

FUCK YOU, KENNY. AN' IF HE PULLS HIS, YOU OPEN F

AND HELL FOLLOWED WITH HIM

GARTH ENNIS
WRITER

STEVE DILLON
ARTIST

MATT HOLLINGSWORTH - COLORIST

CLEM ROBINS - LETTERER

JULIE ROTTENBERG - ASSOC. EDITOR

STUART MOORE - EDITOR

PREACHER CREATED BY

GARTH ENNIS and STEVE DILLON

ASK ME, SHOULD BE AGENT DINNINGS EXTENDING US SOME FUCKIN' COURTESY AN' TELLING US WHAT HIS GODDAMN *EFF BEE AYE* GENETIC SCIENTISTS'VE LET LOOSE ON US...

JESUS, HUGO--

MOTHERFUCKERS'VE BUILT A FELLA CAN MAKE YOU DO WHATEVER HE SAYS, AN' A SON OF A BITCH COP KILLER *ROBOT* THEY'VE LET LOOSE ON US--

HUGO!

I GOT THE PROOF RIGHT HERE. SHAMPOO *AND* CONDITIONER? FUCK NO, COP'S BLOOD--

OKAY HUGO --

THANKS FOR YOUR 'TIME. WE GOT YOUR REPORT, WE'LL LET YOU KNOW AS SOON AS ANY OF THESE SUSPECTS ARE SIGHTED.

GET ON HOME AND GET SOME REST, HUH?

JESUS--!

SWEET GUY.

FUCK HIM. WHAT YOU MAKE OF ANNVILLE?

WELL, GOING BY WHAT I SAW THERE ON MY WAY DOWN, I'D SAY SOMEONE PACKED THE WHOLE POPULATION INTO THE CHURCH AN' THEN LAID IN TEN GALLONS OF NAPALM ...

THAT YOUR THEORY?

IT'S A THEORY.

GOTTA BE BETTER THAN SHERIFF GOODOLEBOY'S, HASN'T IT?

59

ARE YOU GETTING ANY MORE FROM THE THING IN YOUR HEAD...?

KIND OF.

FIRST OFF, I FEEL LIKE IT'S...SHIT, IT'S *BECOMING* ME. IT AIN'T MUCH MORE THAN AN IDEA WRAPPED AROUND A SHIT-LOAD OF POWER --BOTH OF WHICH'RE BECOMING *MINE*.

AND I THINK I'M HEARING ITS NAME, ONE WORD, REPEATED OVER AND OVER IN MY HEAD...

GENESIS.

WELL...YOUR HAVING THIS THING SEEMS TO COINCIDE WITH YOUR CHURCH BEING BLOWN TO BITS...

BUT GENESIS, THAT MAKES YOU THINK MORE OF *CREATION* ...BIRTH, OR THE FIRST BOOK OF THE BIBLE--

OR A FUCKIN' TERRIBLE BAND.

AAAH!

COULDN'T RESIST.

NOW THAT *IS* NICE. SODDIN' EXPENSIVE, LIKE.

HE CAN PAY ME BACK.

OH, AYE.

OKAY, LOOK: I'M HELPING HIM BECAUSE I WANT TO KNOW *WHY* HE LEFT ME WITHOUT A GODDAMN WORD AND BECAME *MINISTER* OF SOME SHIT-HOLE IN THE ASS-END OF TEXAS. AND THAT'S *ALL*.

WHAT'S YOUR EXCUSE?

FOR CHRIST'S SAKE, IT'S CAUSE I'M FUCKIN' FASCINATED!

YOU SAW WHAT HE DID TO THE COPS, DIDN'T YOU? IF HE CAN DO THAT SORT'VE THING ON A REGULAR BASIS, THE SKY'S GONNA BE THE FUCKIN' LIMIT!

JUST IMAGINE:

"MS. CRAWFORD, MS. SCHIFFER--SMEAR MY HANDSOME IRISH FRIEND IN SOUTHERN COMFORT AN' THEN LICK IT ALL OFF. MR. JAGGER, YOU LOAD KEITH'S COKE INTO THE BACK OF THAT *747*. THEN SIGN THIS CHECK.

EXCUSE ME?

I HAVE TO CLOSE UP--

SURE. SORRY.

UH, DO YOU SELL THOSE LITTLE METAL THINGS? LIKE YOU PUT ON THE TIPS OF SHIRT COLLARS?

PLUS: I CAN'T WAIT TO SEE YOU EXPLAIN TO HIM ABOUT THE *GUN* YOU'VE GOT IN YOUR HANDBAG...

DEBLANC...?

HELLO, FIORE.

WHAT'RE YOU--ARE YOU DRUNK?

I TELL YOU WHAT: YOU GIVE ME WHATEVER MESSAGE IT IS YOU CAME TO GIVE ME, AND I'LL TELL YOU WHY I'M GETTING SO ARSEHOLED.

MM-HMMM...

WHY?!

THE SAINT HAS KILLED PILO AND ABOUT A DOZEN MORTALS--

IMAGINE THAT. THE PATRON SAINT OF MURDERERS AND ASSASSINS HAS BEEN KILLING PEOPLE.

FIORE, I DON'T CARE IF THE BODYCOUNT REACHES TRIPLE FIGURES. WE SENT HIM BECAUSE NOTHING'LL STOP HIM GETTING GENESIS BACK.

IT'S NOT JUST THAT! HIS INVOLVEMENT PROVES OURS! HAD YOU CONSIDERED THAT?

SURE I CONSIDERED IT. BUT THAT'S NOT WHY I'M DRINKING.

I'M DRINKING BECAUSE SOONER OR LATER THE GRAIL ARE GONNA HEAR ABOUT THIS.

OH FUCK.

I THINK I NEED A DRINK.

SO, PREACHER-- YOU DON'T MIND ME CALLIN' YOU PREACHER, DO YOU?

WELL, I'M STILL WEARIN' THE COLLAR. I'LL LET YOU KNOW WHEN YOU START PISSIN' ME OFF.

SO, PREACHER --WHAT NEXT?

BEEN THINKIN' ON IT. I GOT THAT GUNFIGHTER SON OF A BITCH AFTER ME AN' PROBABLY THE COPS TOO -- AN' UNTIL I GET A BETTER IDEA WHAT *GENESIS* WANTS IN MY HEAD, I GOT A WHOLE OTHER SET OF PROBLEMS RIGHT THERE.

NOW I APPRECIATE THE HELL OUT'VE WHAT YOU BOTH BEEN DOIN' FOR ME, BUT IT'S GETTIN' A LITTLE ABOVE AN' BEYOND. I FIGURE FROM HERE ON IN I'M ON MY OWN.

AW, COME ON!

YOU LEFT ME BEHIND *BEFORE*, REMEMBER? UNTIL I HEAR THE REASON WHY--

'SCUSE ME?

I BRUNG YOUR CHANGE. YOU A *REAL* PREACHER?

WHAT WOULD A REAL ONE BE DOIN' IN A DEN OF SIN LIKE THIS?

GO ON AN' KEEP IT, HONEY.

71

73

YOU THINK THAT'S ALL IT IS? OKAY, LET'S SEE WHAT HAPPENS WHEN THE GRAIL FIND OUT ABOUT GENESIS! LET'S SEE THE SERAPHI DEAL WITH THE BATTLE OF ARMAGEDDON!

THE GRAIL COULDN'T START *THAT*--!

COULDN'T THEY? THEY'VE GOT PEOPLE *EVERYWHERE*, FIORE. EARS TO THE WALLS. FINGERS ON BUTTONS.

AND REMEMBER, ALL THEY WANT IS AN EXCUSE TO GET STARTED. AFTER TWO THOUSAND YEARS OF PRESERVING A SINGLE BLOODLINE, THEY'RE BOUND TO BE A LITTLE IMPATIENT FOR THE OFF...

WHY'D YOU THINK I SENT *PILO* TO WAKE THE SAINT? TO CERTAIN DEATH?

YOU'RE NOT SUGGESTING PILO WAS A SPY FOR THE GRAIL?

HE WAS TOO EAGER FOR MY LIKING. TOO CLEAN-CUT. TOO GOOD TO BE TRUE.

HE WAS AN ANGEL OF THE LORD! WHAT'D YOU EXPECT HIM TO DO, DEAL CRACK?

PILO WASN'T A SPY...!

WELL THEN HE WAS JUST A FUCKING LITTLE CRAWLER, AND HE DESERVED IT ANYWAY.

DON'T WORRY ABOUT IT, FIORE. WE'RE ALL GONNA GET WHAT'S COMING TO US.

BELIEVE YOU ME...

THE KINGDOM OF HEAVEN IS *FUCKED*.

ULK-ULK-ULK--

JESSE, SAY SOMETHING!

AAHHHHH!

THAT HIT THE SPOT!

FUCK YOU DO THAT FOR?

I WAS HUNGRY.

SO YOU FIGURED YOU'D SNACK ON THIS FELLA'S NECK?

SHIT--!

THIS WHY YOU SLEEP ALL DAY? OUT OF THE SUN?

SPOT ON. IF I CATCH A FEW RAYS, I EXPLODE LIKE SIX TONS OF SEMTEX.

HE'S... HE'S A ...

THE "V" WORD.

FOR FUCK'S SAKE!!

I TOLD YOU NOT TO DO THAT AGAIN! NOBODY TELLS ME WHAT TO DO! AN' I DON'T KNOW IF YOU NOTICED, BUT THAT WEE SHITE STUCK A KNIFE IN MY EYE!!

THAT DON'T MAKE HIM A TWO-DOLLAR SLURPEE! AN' I'D'VE TOLD YOU TO FUCK YOURSELF THE MINUTE I SET EYES ON YOU, I'D KNOWN YOU FOR A FUCKIN' ABOMINATION!

AND THE HORSE YOU RODE IN ON

GARTH ENNIS – WRITER
STEVE DILLON – ARTIST
MATT HOLLINGSWORTH – COLORIST
CLEM ROBINS – LETTERER
JULIE ROTTENBERG – ASSOC. EDITOR
STUART MOORE – EDITOR
PREACHER CREATED BY
GARTH ENNIS and STEVE DILLON

HATE TO SAY IT, BUT IT LOOKS LIKE HUGO WASN'T CUCKOO AFTER ALL...

POSITIVE I.D.?

GOOD ENOUGH.

...THEN THE TALL ONE, THE ONE DRESSED LIKE A REVER'ND, HE QUITS BEATIN' ON ME AN' I LOOK UP AN' THERE'S THE UGLY FELLA *BITIN' INTO HORACE'S NECK AN' DRINKIN' HIS GODDAMN BLOOD--*

YOU CALL THAT GOOD? YOU GONNA ASK BRAM STOKER THERE TO TESTIFY?

DESCRIPTIONS MATCH HUGO'S, IS THE POINT.

GIRL AN' THE, *UH,* BLOODSUCKIN' INDIVIDUAL, WE'RE STILL COMIN' UP EMPTY. OTHER ONE *MIGHT* BE ONE REV-EREND CUSTER, MINISTER OF THE CHURCH IN ANNVILLE.

THE CHURCH THAT WAS BURNT TO THE GROUND, YOU MEAN?

JUST BONES LEFT. CAN'T TELL IF CUSTER WAS IN WITH 'EM 'TIL THEY PULL THE DENTAL RECORDS FOR TWO HUNDRED CITIZENS.

CARLINGTON FAXED US A PICTURE. FELLA OVER THERE SAYS IT'S *KINDA* LIKE HIS ASSAILANT. AND THE COLLAR, TOO...

"GOOD ENOUGH." "COMIN' UP EMPTY." "MIGHT BE." "KINDA."

WANT MY OFFICERS TO LOOK THE OTHER WAY WHILE YOU TAKE A SHOT AT FUCKING YOURSELF?

YOU GOTTA ADMIT THAT THIS IS GETTIN' MORE FUCKED-UP BY THE MINUTE...

YEAH, I'M ABOUT TO CALL MY BUDDY WORKS ON THE X-FILES. LEMME SEE THAT, HUH?

SHERIFF MEEKER? SIR?

JUST HEARD: 911 CALL CAME IN TEN MINUTES AGO FROM THAT TRUCKSTOP WEST OF DEERFORTH. SOMETHIN' ABOUT SHOOTIN', AN' A GUY SOUNDS LIKE SHERIFF ROOT'S COP KILLER...

AND?

GOT CUT OFF.

GET 'EM READY TO GO, DOBIE.

YOU'RE REALLY BUYIN' THIS, HUH?

RECKON I AM.

BETH, CALL CARLINGTON AN' GET TACTICAL OUT TO THE TEN-TEN BAR. TELL 'EM TO PROCEED WITH EXTREME CAUTION -- I'LL FILL 'EM IN ON THE WAY.

'FORE YOU PATCH ME THROUGH TO 'EM, THOUGH:

GET ME HUGO ROOT.

84

SHUHH WUHH WUH CUHFUHH TUHGUH UH TUHVUH FUHHED, DUH!*

*SURE WISH WE COULD AFFORD TO GET THE T.V. FIXED, DAD!

MUHH BUH RUHUHUHHUHH BUHH SHUHHH! BUHH, UH WUH UH CUHH CUHHLUHHUHWUH UH YUHH CUH! YUHH THUH UH CUH BUH YUH DUHPUH WUH DUH, DUHH?*

*MUST BE REAL EXCITING BEING A SHERIFF! BOY, I WISH I COULD COME ALONG ON ONE OF YOUR CASES! YOU THINK I COULD BE YOUR DEPUTY ONE DAY, DAD?

FUHUHSUH LUHMUH! MUH WUHHH YUH BUHH! WHUHH TUHH WHUHBUH, UH?*

*FATHER AND SON LAWMEN! 'ME WATCHIN' YOUR BACK! WHAT A TEAM WE'D BE, HUH?

HUGO ROOT HERE!

BUHH, DUHUHVUH HUHH UH RUH!*

*BOY, I DIDN'T EVEN HEAR IT RING!

MEEKER, YOU AIN'T INTERRUPTIN' PUCKIN' SHIT--

WHAT? YEAH?

AIN'T THAT WHAT I FUCKIN' TOLD YOU?

85

ALL OF 'EM?

THEY'RE LEAVING TWO DEPUTIES, AND THE SECOND AMBULANCE HASN'T CLOSED UP YET...BUT YEAH, THE REST'RE GONE.

I STILL DON'T LIKE BEING HERE, JESSE. LET'S GO, MM?

WE ONLY JUST BROKE IN...LOOK, WE'RE BOTH BEAT. WON'T HURT TO LIE LOW FOR A COUPLA HOURS.

YEAH, BUT WE NEED TO TALK...

OKAY. THAT TRUE ABOUT THE GUN IN YOUR HANDBAG?

I DIDN'T MEAN THAT--

SO WE DON'T NEED TO TALK ABOUT IT, HUH?

87

WHAT'RE YOU SMILING FOR?

YOU AIN'T CHANGED MUCH EITHER.

WHAT'S THAT SUPPOSED TO MEAN?

WELL, THIS IS THE OLDEST, DUMBEST LINE THERE IS. JUST HAPPENS THAT IT'S ALWAYS BEEN TRUE FOR YOU:

YOU AIN'T NEVER PRETTIER'N WHEN YOU'RE ANGRY.

WELL-- YOU'LL BE PLEASED TO HEAR YOU'VE GOT ME FEELING REAL PRETTY. MY WHOLE LIFE'S TURNED TO SHIT BECAUSE OF YOUR FUCKING GENESIS--

KEEP SCOWLIN' TULIP. YOU'RE PROVIN' MY POINT.

SCREW YOURSELF. THANKS TO YOU I'M A FUGITIVE FROM JUSTICE, I'M FLAT BROKE--

AND I KISSED YOU.

WHAT?

WHEN YOU PULLED ME OUT OF ANNVILLE, REMEMBER? THAT MUST'VE PISSED YOU OFF CONSIDERABLY.

JESSE, DON'T.

IF YOU'VE GOT ANY DECENT FEELINGS AT ALL FOR ME, PLEASE DON'T.

CAREFUL YOU DON'T HIT YOUR HEAD ON THE BATHROOM CABINET. IT'S RIGHT OVER THE SINK--

AAH, FUCK!

FOUND IT, HUH?

TOLD YOU, YOU SHOULD'VE PUT THE LIGHTS ON. NO ONE WOULD'VE SEEN US.

...

JESSE?

95

YOU GONNA WORK A WEREWOLF INTO THIS? COUPLE OF TROLLS?

YOU GOT FELLAS LIKE CASSIDY, WHY NOT ANGELS AN' DEMONS?

POINT IS, THEY WEREN'T MEANT TO BE DOIN' IT. THEY GOT CAUGHT.

HEAVEN AN' HELL'RE AT WAR WITH EACH OTHER. THESE TWO BROKE THE RULES WHEN THEY FELL IN LOVE. THEY... GOT KILLED FOR IT.

BUT THE KID THE GIRL HAD, THAT WAS GENESIS. AN' IT'S SOMETHING NEVER HAPPENED BEFORE -- A MIX OF DEMON AND ANGEL, A NEW IDEA...

GOOD AND EVIL TOGETHER?

HEAVEN AN' HELL. GOT A FEELIN' THEY AIN'T NECESSARILY THE SAME THINGS.

BUT BECAUSE GENESIS WAS A NEW IDEA, IT WAS AS POWERFUL AS EITHER'VE THE OLD ONES. YOU WERE TALKIN' ABOUT THE WORD OF GOD, AN' I GOT A FEELIN' YOU WERE RIGHT.

THIS THING I GOT:

I THINK IT'S AS STRONG AS GOD ALMIGHTY.

NEXT: THE REVELATION

TELL ME, DOCTOR CASSIDY: HOW WOULD YOU TREAT A LARGE CALIBER GUNSHOT WOUND RESULTING IN MASSIVE TISSUE AND BLOOD LOSS?

"WELL, I WOULD OBVIOUSLY RECOMMEND DRINKING A COUPLE OF MORONS' WORTH OF FRESH BLOOD AND LETTING THE WOUND HEAL UP BY ITSELF..."

"BUT I WOULD FIRST ADVISE THE PATIENT TO FIND THAT SAINT OF KILLERS FUCKER AND DRIVE A PICKUP TRUCK UP THE BASTARD'S ARSE AT TOP SPEED."

AND WHAT PURPOSE WOULD THAT SERVE, DOCTOR?

"WELL, IT WOULD FIRST OF ALL HELP THE PATIENT TO FEEL MORE POSITIVE, A VITAL STEP ON THE ROAD TO RECOVERY..."

"AND IT WOULD ALSO SAVE ONE REVEREND JESSE CUSTER FROM CERTAIN DEATH AT THE HANDS OF SAID FUCKER."

BUT DOCTOR: JESSE CUSTER FORCED THE PATIENT TO STOP DRINKING THAT STUPID SHITKICKER'S BLOOD, AND THEN WENT ON TO CALL HIM AN ABOMINATION...

"YES, BUT CAREFUL CONSIDERATION WILL REVEAL THAT JESSE IS NOT A BAD BLOKE REALLY, AND TEMPERS WERE PRETTY HEATED ALL ROUND. AND IF THE PATIENT DOESN'T HELP, HE KNOWS HE'LL FEEL BAD FOR AT LEAST A YEAR."

YOU'RE A RIGHT MAD BASTARD, DOCTOR CASSIDY.

I'M GLAD I CAME TO YOU.

113

HE QUIT.

...

AIN'T QUITE THE ANSWER I EXPECTED. FUCK D'YOU MEAN, *HE QUIT?*

HE'S GONE. HE CAME TO US ONE DAY, ALL OF HIS ANGELS, AND HE SAID HE HAD TO GO ON A JOURNEY TO EARTH. HE LEFT STRAIGHT AWAY, AND HE HASN'T BEEN HEARD FROM SINCE.

HE LEFT HEAVEN IN THE CHARGE OF THE *SERAPHI*, THE WARRIOR ARCHANGELS WHO SIT AT THE RIGHT OF HIS THRONE.

HOW THE HELL CAN *GOD QUIT...?*

WE ADEPHI ARE SCIENTISTS, LESSER ANGELS... ACTUALLY, WE DO ALL THE REAL WORK. BUT THE LONG AND THE SHORT OF IT IS:

HE QUIT.

114

OKAY, LOOK: YOU'VE FOUND US OUT, BUT WHO'S GOING TO *BELIEVE* YOU?

YOU'VE GOT THE SAME PROBLEM WE ALWAYS HAVE: THE *ATHEISTS*. START TELLING PEOPLE GOD'S NOT THERE, AND YOU'LL GET THE SAME BLANK STARES YOU GOT WHEN YOU SAID HE *WAS*...

REMEMBER ANNVILLE, REVEREND CUSTER?

IT'S NOT TOO LATE TO FIX ALL THIS. WE CAN ISOLATE THE GENESIS ENTITY FROM YOUR SOUL. WE KNOW HOW TO.

COME ON...

YOU CAN'T JUST WANDER THE WORLD WITH A POWER AS STRONG AS THE *LORD'S*.

IT *IS* AS STRONG AS HIM, HUH?

AH-- WELL--

RECKON YOU'RE RIGHT. NO ONE'S GONNA BELIEVE *ANY OF THIS* --UNLESS THEY HEAR IT FROM THE LORD HIMSELF...

YOU KNOW WHAT? I'M GONNA GO LOOKIN' FOR HIM. I DON'T CARE HOW LONG IT TAKES OR WHERE I HAVE TO GO. I'M GONNA *FIND HIM*.

AN' I'M GONNA *MAKE HIM* TELL HIS PEOPLE WHAT HE'S DONE.

117

FIGURE WE MISSED ALL THE ACTION HERE, TOO.

IF IT WAS ANYTHING LIKE THE ACTION AT THE TEN-TEN, I'M NOT TOO UNHAPPY ABOUT THAT.

YOU KNOW, EVER SINCE I CROSSED THE MASON-DIXON I'VE BEEN DRINKING UNIFORMLY SHITTY COFFEE. OR DID YOU GET ALL EXCITED AGAIN?

BLOW ME. HEY, THIS OUGHTA BE TOUCHING...

UH MUH DUH GUHBUH UKAH?*

*IS MY DAD GONNA BE OKAY?

WELL, UH--

LOOK, NO OFFENSE, BUT IS THERE ANY CHANCE YOU COULD FACE THE OTHER WAY WHILE I'M TALKING TO YOU? YOUR FACE IS MAKING ME NAUSEOUS, IS ALL.

SHUH THUH!*

*SURE THING!

THANKS.

LOOK, YOUR FATHER'S SEVERED PENIS IS STUCK IN HIS COLON. IT'S AN HOUR TOO LATE FOR MICROSURGERY, BUT AT LEAST HE'S STABLE...

WE'RE TAKING HIM TO THE HOSPITAL NOW--

S...SON...?

DUHH!*

*DAD!

118

119

A DOZEN MILES FROM DALLAS:

UH MUH HUH *VUHHYUH UH JUHH CUHH! VUHHYUH FUH UH BLUH UH MUH FUHH! UH UH UH HUH UH FUH LUH UH UHH-- SUH BUH UH!*

UH MUH BECUHH UHHFUHH!

*I WILL HAVE *VENGEANCE* ON JESSE CUSTER! VENGEANCE FOR THE BLOOD OF MY FATHER! AND IF I HAVE A FACE LIKE AN ARSE-- *SO BE IT!*

I WILL BECOME *ARSEFACE!*

SAN FRANCISCO:

STRANGE GOINGS- ON DOWN SOUTH, MY LORD.

NOTHING TO DO WITH US, HARCOURT. NOW HAND ME THAT JAR AND GO FIND BOB AND FREDDY, WILL YOU?

LOUISIANA-TEXAS BORDER:

OH, JESSE. OH, YOU'VE GONE AND STRAYED AGAIN.

GRAN'MA DOESN'T LIKE THAT...

LE SAINT-MARIE, SOUTHERN FRANCE:

ENOUGH FOR THE GRAIL TO TAKE AN INTEREST, THIERRY. KEEP ME INFORMED.

TWO NIGHTS LATER WE'VE HITCHED AS FAR AS HOUSTON.

CASSIDY WAS GONE 'TIL DAWN THE FIRST NIGHT, WHEN HE CAME BACK WITH NEW SHADES, MEAT BETWEEN HIS TEETH AND ALL HIS WOUNDS HEALED UP.

FIGURED I'D ASK NO QUESTIONS. HE STUCK BY ME.

TULIP, WELL, I STILL DON'T KNOW WHY SHE'S CARRYIN' A GUN--BUT SHE DON'T KNOW WHY I LEFT HER FOR THE CHURCH.

CHILDISH? SHE STARTED IT.

THREE DAYS TOPS 'TIL I GET HER INTO BED.

ONE THING WORRYIN' ME IS THE SAINT OF KILLERS, OUT THERE WAITIN' FOR HIS CHANCE. AIN'T USIN' THE WORD ON HIM THAT SCARES ME:

IT'S LOOKIN' IN HIS EYES WHILE I TRY.

BUT HE WON'T STOP ME. GONNA FIND THE LORD IF IT TAKES ME A LIFE-TIME.

SO JUST BEFORE I REACH THE DINER, JOHN WAYNE APPEARS OUT OF NOWHERE AND THROWS ME THIS BIG, SHIT-EATING GRIN...

AND I TURN AROUND AND THROW IT RIGHT BACK.

STANDING TALL

GARTH ENNIS – WRITER

STEVE DILLON – ARTIST

MATT HOLLINGSWORTH – COLORIST

CLEM ROBINS – LETTERER

JULIE ROTTENBERG – ASSOC. EDITOR

STUART MOORE – EDITOR

PREACHER CREATED BY

GARTH ENNIS and STEVE DILLON

DIRTY HARRY'S PARTNERS HAVE NOTHING ON ME...

OFF THE FIRE ESCAPE, FUCKO.

MY ONE PIECE OF GOOD LUCK IS MY PARTNER, PAULIE BRIDGES. TOUGH, SMART, SUCCESSFUL, SAVED MY LIFE A HALF-DOZEN TIMES...

SUPERCOP.

WHY YOU FUCKIN' WITH MYMFF!

WHY'D YOU RUN?

YOU FUCKIN' PIG MOTHERFUCKER, LOOK WHAT YOU DID TO MY HOMIE! HE GOT NO FUCKIN' FACE!

TAKE YOUR FUCKIN' PIG HANDS OFF ME, MAN!

WAKEY-- WAKEY!

WHAT... WHAT'STH...

JESUSTH, WHAT'STH GOING ON?!

WHAT'S IT LOOK LIKE?

aaah!

I... I DUNNO. LASTH THING I...I WAS IN HOULIHAN'STH, AND...YOU...

I WAS TALKING TO YOU, RIGHT. YOU JUST GOT OFF WORK. YOU HAD THREE SCREW-DRIVERS, YOU WENT TO THE RESTROOM...

YEAH--

AND WHILE YOU WERE GONE, I SLIPPED A VALIUM INTO YOUR FOURTH.

NOW: YOU KNOW WHAT THIS IS?

SO ARE YOU NOT A WEE BIT WORRIED THEY'RE GONNA TWIG YOU DIDN'T GO UP IN FLAMES WITH THE REST OF YER FLOCK? THERE'S MORE'N LIKELY AN A.P.B. OUT ON YOU BY NOW.

BUT YOU WERE KIND OF INDISCREET FOR A DEAD MAN, WEREN'T YOU? MUST'VE BEEN A DOZEN PEOPLE SAW YOU BEFORE WE LEFT THE STATE. YOU WERE ON FIRST-NAME TERMS WITH THAT TRUCKER BEFORE WE HIT THE MISSISSIPPI...

WHOLE LOT OF JESSES IN THE SOUTH. 'SIDES, HE WAS SO FUCKIN' STONED HE'S FORGOTTEN EVER SEEIN' US, NEVER MIND GIVIN' US A RIDE.

HOW? JUST BONES LEFT.

FIGURE I'LL BE OKAY.

BULLSHIT. YOU'RE ACTING WAY TOO BLASÉ ABOUT THIS, YOU KNOW. YOU'RE PRACTICALLY A FUGITIVE.

TURNIP'S RIGHT--

TULIP.

WHAT YOU SHOULD'VE DONE WAS TO GRAB A FED BEFORE WE LEFT AN' PUT THE WORD ON HIM. END OF A.P.B.

FOR ONCE WE AGREE.

MAYBE. JUST WANTED TO GET OUTTA TEXAS.

THAT BECAUSE DALLAS WAS GETTIN' A LITTLE HOT?

OH, IT'S TIME TO *TALK*, IS IT? WELL, LET'S START WITH WHY I WAS LEFT HIGH AND DRY IN PHOENIX FIVE YEARS AGO--

HIGH AND--? *YOU* HAD THE GODDAMN MONEY!

TWENTY-SEVEN BUCKS! I WENT HOME ON A FUCKING FREIGHT TRAIN!

GUESS THAT'S WHY YOU TURNED TO A LIFE OF CRIME--

CHILDREN, CHILDREN! FUCKSAKE!

MY MATE'LL BE HERE IN A MINUTE, REMEMBER? BE NICE.

... WHAT'S HE CALLED AGAIN?

SI. YOU'LL LIKE HIM. FUCKIN' SPACE-CADET.

HE WRITES FREELANCE FOR A LOT'VE THINGS, BUT HE'S GOT THIS OBSESSION WITH WEIRD SHIT --Y'KNOW, GHOSTS AN' FLYIN' SAUCERS AN' ALL. HE MIGHT HAVE SOME INFO ON THE FELLA YE'RE LOOKIN' FOR.

A U.F.O. FANATIC IS GONNA HELP US *FIND* GOD?

HE LIKES RELIGIOUS PHENOMENA BEST. WEEPIN' STATUES, STIGMATA, VISIONS OF THE VIRGIN. THE GOOD LORD'LL MAYBE'VE SHOWN UP IN THE STUFF SI COLLECTS, AN' I CAN ASK HIM ABOUT IT WITHOUT COMIN' RIGHT OUT AN' SAYIN' WHAT WE'RE UP TO.

BUT IF YOU'VE GOT A BETTER IDEA, I'M FUCKIN' DYIN' TO HEAR IT. MY ROUND.

GUY CAN HELP, I'M HEARIN' HIM OUT. I AIN'T FUCKIN' AROUND WITH THIS THING, OKAY?

JUST DON'T TELL HIM YOUR NAME.

YOUR MOM STILL CHARGE A NICKEL FOR HEAD?

NAH. IT'S BEEN A DIME SINCE I KICKED ALL HER TEETH OUT.

ALL I GOT'S A NICKEL...

NICKEL GETS YOU MY DA.

THEN I'LL STICK TO MY SISTER--

MOTHERFUCKERRRR!!

YOU SON OF A BITCH, YOU FUCKER! HOW YA DOIN,' MAN?

AH, YE FUCKIN' REPROBATE! HOW'RE YOU, YE BASTARD?

YOU MOTHERFUCKER! FUCK, AM I GLAD TO SEE YOU...!

THE AIR'S GONE BLUE...

IT'S A GUY THING.

135

SI, THIS IS TULIP AN' JESSE. I'LL GET YOU A DRINK.

HI.

PLEASED TO MEET YOU, TULIP. JEEZ, IS THAT COLLAR FOR REAL?

YEP.

SHIT, SORRY ABOUT THE LANGUAGE--

AIN'T ANY KIND OF SIN IN MY BOOK.

THAT'S A RELIEF. ah, IT'S JUST I HAVEN'T SEEN THE BASTARD IN FIVE YEARS, Y'KNOW?

LUCKY MAN.

CASS MAKES AN IMPRESSION, DOESN'T HE?

J.D. AN' ICE. SO HOW'S THINGS?

JESUS...BUSY AS SHIT, I TELL YOU. IT WASN'T 'TIL I STOPPED AND THOUGHT ABOUT IT JUST LAST WEEK, I'M FUCKIN' LIVIN' THE MYTH OF THE WORLD-WEARY JOURNALIST.

MY EDITORS ARE SCREAMIN' AT ME FOR SHIT THAT WAS DUE YESTER-DAY, MY APARTMENT'S KNEE-DEEP IN BOTTLES AN' CIGARETTE PACKETS, I CAN'T GET TO THE BEER IN THE REFRIGERATOR 'CAUSE OF ALL THE GODDAMN HALF-EATEN GARBAGE...

GOOD NEWS IS, I AIN'T GOT RATS. BAD NEWS IS, THE ROACHES ATE THE MOTHER-FUCKERS.

ARE YOU STILL FREELANCE, AYE? WHAT'RE YOU WORKIN' ON?

OH, YOU'LL LIKE THIS...

THE REAVER-CLEAVER.

136

SAY WHAT?

YOU AIN'T SEEN THIS ON TV?

uh-uh.

FUCKIN' PRICELESS. OKAY, TWO WEEKS BACK SOME SICK FUCK STARTS KIDNAPPING PEOPLE, SENDING IDENTIFIABLE BITS OF 'EM TO THEIR RELATIVES-- HANDS, JAWS, LIKE THAT.

SOME ASSHOLE AT THE NEWS' DUBS HIM *THE REAVER.* GUESS YOU'VE GOT TO CALL HIM SOMETHING... PROBLEM IS, OVER AT THE *POST,* ASSHOLE *TWO* DECIDES ON *THE CLEAVER.* NEITHER PAPER GIVES IN. AND...

THE REAVER-FUCKIN' CLEAVER...!

LEAVE IT TO REAVER.

HEY, THERE IT IS! IT'S ON!

WHAT, THAT'S HIM...?

JESUS, NO. THAT'S THE COPS THEY GOT HUNTING HIM.

DETECTIVES TOOL AND BRIDGES, PART OF THE *TASK FORCE* SET UP TO FIND THE KILLER.

JESUS, THEY PRACTICALLY *ARE* THE GODDAMN TASK FORCE. NONE'VE THE VICTIMS'VE BEEN TOO IMPORTANT JUST YET. GUY DOES A YUPPIE OR SOME RICH VILLAGE ART-FAG, WATCH 'EM ASSIGN HALF THE FUCKIN' N.Y.P.D.

YOU MET 'EM?

YEAH. NO HELP AT ALL. TOOL'S KINDA DULL, BRIDGES...WELL, HE'S NONE TOO KEEN ON REPORTERS. BUT HE'S A FUCKIN' TOP COP. THEY EVER GET A MOVIE OUT OF IT, SCHWARZENEGGER'S GONNA PLAY HIM.

LISTEN, I'M SORRY ABOUT EARLIER--

WHAT'RE THOSE TWO TALKING ABOUT?

SI LOOKIN' FOR GOD FOR US. HE FIGURES IT'S A PRIVATE FAVOR TO CASS, HE WON'T ASK ANY QUESTIONS.

YOU THINK HE WOULD ANYWAY?

WOULDN'T LIKE TO TRY LYIN' TO HIM. HE'S A SMART GUY, YOU CAN SEE IT IN HIS EYES.

SO LIKE I SAY--

WELL... SURE. WE GOT THE SAME SENSE OF HUMOR--

YEP. CHILDISH AND SICK.

YOU AND "CASS" GOT AWFULLY FRIENDLY AWFULLY QUICK, DIDN'T YOU?

LOOK, I'M TRYNNA APOLOGIZE HERE. YOU AIN'T MAKIN' IT TOO EASY ON ME, Y'KNOW?
I DIDN'T MEAN TO START UP ABOUT WHAT YOU WERE DOIN' IN DALLAS. AN' I *WILL* EXPLAIN WHY I LEFT YOU BEFORE, SOON, BUT IT'S KIND OF HARD 'CAUSE IT HAS TO DO WITH SHIT I DON'T LIKE TO TALK ABOUT...

OKAY?

OKAY, SURE. THAT'S REASONABLE.

HEY, LISTEN: WHEN WE GET BACK TO THE HOTEL? LET'S CHECK OUT OF THE SINGLE ROOMS AND GET A DOUBLE INSTEAD. WE'VE...GOT SOME CATCHING UP TO DO.

YEAH?

IN YOUR DREAMS.

138

HEY, LISTEN, I'M SORRY I GOTTA LEAVE RIGHT NOW BUT I GOT A TON OF SHIT I GOTTA DO. I'LL SEE YOU GUYS AGAIN, OKAY? WHEN I GET CASS'S STUFF OFF THE INTERNET.

SURE. YOU TAKE CARE, SI.

IT WAS NICE MEETING YOU.

uh... INTERNET?

COMPUTER WHIZ KID, TOO. TALENTED BOY WE'VE GOT HERE.

WHAT D'YEZ WANNA DO NOW THEN?

YOUR MOM THINKS SO TOO.

I'LL SEE YOU.

YOU TWO ARE DESPERATE, SO YEZ ARE.

HERE, IT'S ONLY HALF TEN. D'YOU WANT TO COME ON AN' I'LL SHOW YOU ROUND A BIT, AYE?

YOU KNOW THE WAY TO THE EMPIRE STATE BUILDING?

YEAH...LISTEN, THIS IS GONNA SOUND KINDA STUPID:

FUCKIN' TOURIST!

WELL, I'M GONNA GO TURN IN.

HAVE FUN.

141

HE CUHPUHRUHS, ALL RIGHT. HE'S SO CUHPUHRUHTIVE, HE GIVES THE NAME OF HIS SUPPLIER ON THE SPOT. A SOLID GOLD BUST AND IT'S NOT EVEN OUR CASE.

THAT'S WHAT YOU GET WHEN YOU WORK WITH PAULIE BRIDGES.

I MEAN, THAT'S THE ONLY REASON I'M STILL ON THE FORCE. GUY LIKE HIM AS A PARTNER, EVEN A JONAH LIKE ME COMES UP LOOKING GOOD.

WITHOUT HIM, I DON'T THINK I COULD EVEN GET BOUGHT OFF BY THE MOB...

NOT THAT I'D EVER TRY.

PLAY NICE, KIDS.

LIKE FUCKIN' JIM CARREY WITH HIS COCK IN A SOCKET...

THAT BRIDGES, MAN. FUCK.

YOU REMEMBER HE PUSHED THE GUY IN THE--

FUCK YEAH, DIG THIS:

142

ONE EIGHTY SEVEN·IN THE KITCHEN, FALL OF LAST YEAR. BRIDGES TAKES OUT TWO OF THE MOTHERFUCKERS AND THE THIRD ONE QUITS. THEY'RE BRINGIN' OUT THE COP'S BODY JUST WHEN BRIDGES IS CUFFIN' HIS SUSPECT--

NOW, OUR GUY'S GOT IT IN THE STOMACH. TWELVE GAUGE, POINT BLANK. I'M TALKIN' MEAT FEAST AT PIZZA HUT WITH EXTRA PEPPERONI.

BRIDGES SNAPS. HE GETS THE LITTLE BASTARD AND HE STICKS HIS FACE IN THE *GODDAMN* GUNSHOT WOUND.

HOLY SHIT...!

SO WHAT ABOUT HIS PARTNER, UH--

TOOL? HEY, HE ONLY *EXISTS* 'CAUSE BRIDGES WON'T WEAR A BULLETPROOF VEST,!

TOOL'S SUCH A FAGGOT, WHEN HE TORTURES A SUSPECT HE FLUSHES THE GUY'S HEAD IN THE *BIDET.*

YOU WANT TO GRAB A BEER ON THE WAY HOME?

SURE. GETTING A LITTLE LATE TO HUNT OUR BAD GUY, HUH?

FUCK THAT, JOHNNY.

IT'S NEVER TOO LATE.

ALL THEY HAD WAS BUD.

'COURSE, YOU COULD NIP IN THERE AN' ORDER THEM TO GO OUT AN' GET US A MAGNUM OF KRUG AN' THEY'D HAVE TO OBEY YOU, Y'KNOW.

MM.

COME TO THAT, YOU COULD'VE WALKED INTO THE RITZ CARLTON AN' GOTTEN US A COUPLE'VE SUITES, AN' THEN WE WOULDN'T BE STAYIN' IN THAT POKEY WEE HOLE ON SECOND AVENUE...

I COULD'VE.

SO WHY DIDN'T YOU?

'CAUSE THAT JUST AIN'T THE WAY IT WORKS.

144

SO HOW DOES IT WORK, THEN? CHEERS.

COMES DOWN TO RESPONSIBILITY.

THIS OUGHTTA BE GOOD...

I'M LOOKIN' FOR THE LORD 'CAUSE I FIGURE HE'S DESERTED HIS CREATION. I AIM TO BRING HIM TO BOOK FOR THAT LITTLE TRANSGRESSION: TO CONFRONT HIM AND HEAR HIS ANSWER TO THAT CHARGE.

HE HAS A OBLIGATION TO DO RIGHT BY THE WORLD HE'S MADE AN' THE FOLKS HE'S PEOPLED IT WITH. HE QUITS AN' RUNS, HE AIN'T FACIN' UP TO HIS RESPONSIBILITIES.

FIGURE IF I START LORDIN' IT OVER PEOPLE WITH THIS GIFT I GOT, JUST TO MAKE LIFE A LITTLE BIT EASIER, WHO AM I GONNA BE TO TALK ABOUT RESPONSIBILITY?

YOU GOT POWER, YOU GOT TO USE IT RIGHT.

SO DO YOU RECKON THAT HIS CREATION AN' ALL THESE GOOD PEOPLE LIVIN' ON IT ARE WORTH THE TIME AN' EFFORT YOU'RE EXPENDIN' ON THEIR BEHALF?

MATTER OF FACT, CASS--

YES I DO.

I S'POSE THAT ALSO EXPLAINS WHY YOU AN' YER WOMAN THERE HAVE SEPARATE ROOMS...

LIKE I NEEDED REMINDIN'.

GONNA BE A SHOCK FOR YOU TO HEAR THIS, BUT MINISTERS TO SMALL TOWNS IN THE ASS-END OF TEXAS DON'T TEND TO GET A WHOLE LOT OF ACTION...

AN' THERE WAS ME THINKIN' THAT COLLAR WAS A FANNY-MAGNET.

HM?

OH AYE. WHERE I COME FROM, FANNY MEANS--

RIGHT.

ANYHOW, ONLY KIND OF GIRL THE COLLAR EVER ATTRACTED FOR ME WAS THE KIND WANTED TO SETTLE DOWN AGED SEVENTEEN : GOOD, GENTLE, HARDWORKING...

FACE LIKE A BULLDOG LICKIN' PISS OFF A NETTLE...

I TELL YOU, IF ABSOLUTE POWER WAS TO CORRUPT ABSOLUTELY, *THAT* IS THE FIRST ABSOLUTELY CORRUPT GODDAMN THING I WOULD DO.

BUT, ORDERIN' TULIP TO COMMIT A CARNAL ACT AGAINST HER WILL WOULD BE AN UNFORGIVABLE SIN FOR WHICH I WOULD RIGHTLY BURN FOREVER IN THE FIRES OF HELL ...SO UNTIL SHE SEES SENSE, I'LL JUST CONTINUE TO SUFFER THE PAIN OF CELIBACY.

AND A BONER COULD KNOCK A GODDAMN DOOR DOWN.

146

147

ONE'VE THE MANY ADVANTAGES, BELIEVE YOU ME.

PERFECT VISION, NOSE LIKE A BLOODHOUND, TAKES ME FIVE SECONDS TO RUN THE HUNDRED... I CAN DRINK FIFTY PINTS AN' WALK A STRAIGHT LINE, AN' KICK THE SHITE OUT'VE MIKE TYSON WHILE I'M DOIN' IT.

AN' I'LL SHOW YOU SOMETHIN' ELSE:

HUH?

QUICKER'N TAKIN' THE LIFT, PREACHER-MAN! SEE YOU AT THE BOTTOM!

WHAT THE FUCK ARE YOU DOIN'? GET DOWN!

OH GOD, I CAN'T STAND IT ANY LONGER! THE BLOOD! THE KILLING! THE POINTLESS BUTCHERY! LET IT END HERE!

CASSIDY, FOR FUCK'S SAKE!

AAAAAAAAHHHHH!

CASSIDYY!!

...COCK.

SUCKER.

148

IS THIS THE KIND OF SOUND MORAL JUDGMENT YOU USED TO TEACH YOUR FLOCK?

HELL WITH MY FLOCK--

YOU TOOK CARE OF THAT EARLIER.

I DIDN'T HIT THE SON OF A BITCH SO WE COULD STEAL HIS BEER. I HIT HIM 'CAUSE HE CALLED ME A REDNECK MOTHERFUCKER. GOTTA BE A MORE POLITE WAY TO ASK A FELLA TO DRINK UP AT CLOSIN' TIME, AIN'T THERE?

WHAT WE OWE HIM FOR?

TEN PITCHERS... EIGHTY BUCKS.

hh-hmm.

AH, I TAKE IT THAT EMBARRASSED COUGH MEANS YOUR HALF GOES ON THE I.O.U. YOU GAVE ME?

I'LL GET SOME CASH SOON AS I CAN--

RELAX.

HONESTLY, MATE, THAT'S THE LOT. WHATEVER IT IS SHE'S HIDING, YOU'LL HAVE TO GET IT FROM HER.

LOOK, THE SUN'LL NEARLY BE UP OUT THERE. I'LL HAVE TO STAY AN' KIP UNDER ONE'VE THE TABLES. THIS IS SI'S ADDRESS --I'LL SEE YOU THERE AT TEN TONIGHT, OKAY?

TONIGHT AT TEN.

I'LL TELL YOU, THIS DOESN'T HALF GO AGAINST THE GRAIN...

DON'T FORGET THE TIP.

YOU SURE THAT'S ALL YOU REMEMBER ABOUT TULIP..?

I KNOW. I KNOW THAT. I AIMED AT HIM, BUT I MISSED AND GOT THE GUY BESIDE HIM. THEN I HAD TO TAKE OFF--

CAN'T YOU GET SOMEONE ELSE? HE'S SEEN ME, HE KNOWS...LOOK, I'M NOT COMING ALL THE WAY FROM NEW YORK TO DALLAS JUST TO FINISH--

THE JOB...

'SCUSE.

UH--

WELL, IT'S A BIG CITY, MACAVOY. YOU WANT ME, LET'S SEE YOU FIND ME.

OKAY, YEAH, SURE, WHATEVER YOU SAY. YOU'RE THE BOSS.

LET ME JUST GET A PEN--

JUST A SECOND-- OKAY, GOT ONE.

I KNEW IT!

154

GOD DAMMIT...

YOU'VE GOT SOME NERVE, CUSTER! WHAT THE *HELL* GIVES YOU THE RIGHT TO SPY ON ME?

WHO'S GONNA PUT A BULLET IN YOUR HEAD? WHOSE FACE'D YOU BLOW OFF? WHO'D YOU *MISS*? WHAT JOB? WHO'S MACAVOY?

WHAT THE FUCK ARE YOU, SOME KIND OF *CONTRACT KILLER*?!

YOU KIDDIN'?

...WELL, IF IT'S TIME TO TELL ALL, JESSE: AFTER YOU.

YOU EVER GONNA GROW UP, TULIP?

WHAT THE FUCK *DO* YOU MEAN...?

I MEAN, WHEN'RE YOU GONNA STOP PLAYING GAMES AN' ADMIT ALL YOU WANNA DO IS GO TO BED WITH ME?

I'D SOONER FUCK CASSIDY.

HURTS, BUT I'LL BE SURE TO TELL HIM.

DON'T YOU DARE!

WHERE DO YOU GET OFF, SAYING A THING LIKE THAT?

AW, CUT THE HORSESHIT! IF IT AIN'T TRUE, WHY'RE YOU STICKIN' AROUND? WHAT'S KEEPIN' YOU WITH ME?

I TOLD YOU--

YEAH, SURE, SO I'LL TELL YOU WHY I LEFT YOU. GIMME A BREAK: NO ONE GOES THROUGH THE SHIT YOU HAVE RECENTLY JUST TO SATISFY THEIR GODDAMN CURIOSITY!

SAY I DID EXPLAIN--WHAT NEXT? YOU UP AN' LEAVE? "THANKS FOR TELLIN' ME THE BIG SECRET, JESSE, I BEEN DYIN' TO KNOW. THAT'S ALL, YOU GET ON WITH YOUR LIFE NOW."

SO WHAT'S YOUR EXCUSE? WHY'RE YOU SO INTERESTED IN MY SECRET?

HEY, I'M CURIOUS TOO. DIFFERENCE IS, I AIN'T USIN' THE FACT TO COVER UP WHAT I REALLY WANT.

OUT.

NEARLY THERE, PILGRIM.

uh-huh.

BEING THE UNLUCKIEST COP IN THE WORLD, I DON'T GO ON TOO MANY DATES. THE ONE TIME I DID, WE FOUND A PLACE THAT DIDN'T MIND HER SEEING-EYE DOG AND I TOLD HER ABOUT MYSELF.

SHE STARTED TO NOD OFF INTO THE SOUP, SO I CHANGED TACK AND TOLD HER ABOUT PAULIE BRIDGES INSTEAD...

AW--!

CHRISTOPHER ST

I MENTIONED HE LIVED ON CHRISTOPHER STREET, BY HIMSELF. "AH," SHE SAID, AND HER SMILE BECAME A GENTLE SMIRK, LIKE WE WERE SHARING A FUNNY LITTLE SECRET.

WHEN I REALIZED THE CONCLUSION SHE'D JUMPED TO, I LAUGHED SO HARD I CHOKED ON AN OVERSIZED CROUTON.

SHE MUST'VE THOUGHT I WAS LAUGHING AT HER, BECAUSE SHE LEFT BEFORE THE WAITRESS GOT THROUGH WITH THE HEIMLICH MANEUVER...

I TELL YOU, JOHNNY, THIS FUCKIN' STREET MAKES ME WANT TO PUKE...

BUT THAT WASN'T IT.

SHE JUST DIDN'T KNOW PAULIE.

FUCKIN' FAGGOTS EVERYWHERE. JESUS.

OUGHTTA ORGANIZE A CULL.

NEW YORK'S FINEST

GARTH ENNIS — WRITER STEVE DILLON — ARTIST

MATT HOLLINGSWORTH — COLORIST

CLEM ROBINS — LETTERER

JULIE ROTTENBERG — ASSOC EDITOR

STUART MOORE — EDITOR

PREACHER CREATED BY

GARTH ENNIS AND STEVE DILLON

158

159

MEAT-BALLS?

SPECIAL AT THE DELI.

TOOL.

HELLO, DETECTIVE.

IS THAT A FACT? LOOK, THIS MAY BE VERY FUNNY FOR YOU--

IT CERTAINLY IS. IF YOU CAN'T LAUGH AT SEVERED TESTICLES IN THE MAIL, WHAT CAN YOU LAUGH AT?

BRRRNNG

I'M THE KILLER.

NOW SEEING AS THAT JUICY LITTLE DETAIL HASN'T YET BEEN MADE PUBLIC, I FIGURE YOU'RE CONVINCED I'M ON THE LEVEL.

I JUST WANTED TO ESTABLISH THAT FOR WHEN I CALL AGAIN...

IT'S HIM! VENUCCI, I'VE GOT HIM ON THE LINE! TAP IT!

HUH?

HOW THE FUCK CAN I? YOUR PHONE ISN'T HOOKED UP! AND DON'T FUCKING SHOUT AT ME, TOOL!

BUT-- BUT--

'BYE FOR NOW.

...GOD'STH STHAKE, KILL ME...

162

AH, YOU FOUND IT!

NICE NEIGHBORHOOD SI LIVES IN.

AYE, BUT LOOK AT HIS LITTLE ISLAND OF ELEGANCE AND TASTE IN THE MIDDLE OF IT. HE'S AWAY OUT FOR MORE BEER.

SO WHAT'VE YEZ BEEN UP TO?

SEEIN' THE TOWN.

HAVE WE EVER. HE IS SUCH A GODDAMN TOURIST...

AIN'T ASHAMED OF IT, NEITHER. TIMES SQUARE, BATTERY PARK, STATUE OF LIBERTY--SHE WAS SOMETHIN', OUT THERE IN THE WATER WITH THE SUN GOIN' DOWN BEHIND HER...

LOVELY ARSE ON HER, TOO.

KINDA LIPPY FOR TEMPEST-TOSS'D WRETCHED REFUSE OF A FORBIGN SHORE, AIN'T YOU?

YOU'RE RIGHT. I'M JUST A HUMBLE WEE HUDDLED MASS YEARNIN' TO BREATHE FREE.

LISTEN: SI WAS ASKIN' IF THIS STUFF ABOUT SIGHTINGS OF GOD WAS FOR YOU AN' NOT ME, SO I JUST WENT AHEAD AND OWNED UP.

WELL, I DON'T MEAN ABOUT *EVERYTHING!* LOOK, WE GO BACK A LONG WAY TO-GETHER--HE'S NEVER GONNA BELIEVE I GIVE A FUCK WHERE THE LORD'S BEEN SEEN RECENTLY!

I SAID YOU'D LOST YOUR FAITH AND YOU WANTED TO TALK TO SOMEONE WHO'D REALLY SEEN GOD, NOT JUST READ THE BIBLE--

BRILLIANT.

AW, SURE I COULD'VE TOLD HIM THE TRUTH AN' HE WOULDN'T'VE BREATHED A WORD. I TOLD YOU, WE'VE BEEN MATES FOR AGES.

YEAH, *YOU* HAVE. AND HOW LONG IS AGES, EXACTLY?

IF YOU'RE WORRIED ABOUT HIM BITIN' YER NECK, YOU CAN RELAX. I MET HIM AT WOODSTOCK. HE WAS SIXTEEN.

SO WHAT'D YOU TELL HIM?

SOUNDS LIKE HIM NOW...

HI--THANKS. HOW YOU DOIN'?

HEARIN' HOW THE TWO'VE YOU MET UP.

OH, THAT'S SOME STORY...

HELLO AGAIN, TULIP. HI, FUCKRAT.

HOW'RE YEH, SHITEBUCKET? I WAS JUST TALKIN' ABOUT YOU.

I HEARD.

THERE I AM AT WOODSTOCK, AND I'VE JUST TAKEN THE BROWN ACID WHEN THEY COME ON THE P.A. AND SAY, "WHATEVER YOU DO, DON'T TAKE THE BROWN ACID"--

TULIP, CASS DIDN'T KNOW WHAT YOU'D WANT TO DRINK. BEER OKAY?

SHE LIKES COCKTAILS. STICK AN UMBRELLA IN IT.

I WANDER UP THIS HILL IN THE MIDDLE OF THE NIGHT, *OUT OF MY FUCKING MIND*—I WANT TO PUKE SO BAD BUT I'M SCARED EVERYTHING FROM MY TONGUE TO MY ASSHOLE'S GONNA COME UP ALONG WITH IT, AND I'M KEEPING MY MOUTH TIGHT SHUT...

SO YOU CAN IMAGINE HOW I FELT WHEN I SAW *THIS* MOTHERFUCKER, GETTING SHOT IN THE FACE BY A GIANT HELL'S ANGEL.

HE SAID SOMETHIN' ABOUT THE POPE, SO I PISSED ON HIS HARLEY. I ALWAYS GET CATHOLIC ON HEROIN.

HE FALLS ON HIS ASS. THEN HE GETS UP, MINUS HIS HANDSOME FEATURES, AND BUSTS THIS PRICK'S SHOTGUN OVER HIS HEAD.

THEN HE BITES HIS THROAT OPEN AND STARTS DRINKING.

MY FEET HAVE PUT DOWN ROOTS. I *KNOW* I'M IN HELL AND I'VE MET THE DEVIL.

SO HE DUMPS THE STIFF AND COMES OVER, AND I'M TRYING TO EXPLAIN WHAT'S WRONG WITH ME...

ALL HE COULD SAY WAS *BRRROOWWWNNN,* BUT I GOT THE IDEA.

THIS FUCKIN' GUY SITS ON THE HILL BESIDE ME WITH NO FACE ON HIS SKULL AND TALKS ME DOWN FROM THE WORST TRIP OF MY *LIFE.*

I FELT A WEE BIT RESPONSIBLE --UIK--UIK--

A NICE GUY AT HEART, MM?

JUST A RUMOR, ACTUALLY.

GIVE'S ANOTHER BEER.

165

SHAME YOU'RE NOT LOOKING FOR UFOS, JESSE. DIME A DOZEN ROUND THIS TIME OF YEAR.

OKAY...SLIGHT DEARTH OF MANIFESTATIONS BY THE GOOD LORD JUST RIGHT NOW. THEY'RE USUALLY NO GOOD ANYWAY--SOME GOAT-FUCKER IN ARKANSAW SEES JESUS IN THE SUNSET, THAT KIND OF THING...

THE ONLY IDEA I REALLY HAD IS THIS GUY I KNOW IN THE VILLAGE. WEIRD CHARACTER, LOST HIS SIGHT IN AN ACCIDENT. HE STILL GETS ABOUT FINE--NO DOG, NO WHITE STICK, JUST WALKS AROUND AND NEVER HITS A DAMN THING.

HE SAYS GOD GUIDES HIM. GOING BLIND PUT HIM IN TOUCH WITH HIS MAKER. WHAT NEED HAS HE OF EYES WHEN THE HAND OF THE LORD IS ON HIS SHOULDER ET CETERA ET CETERA.

GOT QUITE A FOLLOWING, TOO...

YOU TAKE ME TO HIM?

I CAN TAKE YOU TO HIS PLACE. HE *HATES ME*--I WROTE A PIECE FOR THE *VOICE* ABOUT HIM, SAID HE TOOK A BUDDY ALONG TO WHISPER DIRECTIONS. GOT HIM GOOD AND PISSED.

HOW'D HE READ IT?

heh...ANYWAY, I WROTE IT WITH-OUT ACTUALLY SEEING HIM IN ACTION. TELL YOU THE TRUTH, I HAD TO EAT MY WORDS A LITTLE. I'M ABOUT HALF-CONVINCED.

HE CALLS HIMSELF THE BIG MAN.

THE BIG MAN... WHEN CAN WE GO?

TOMORROW'S GOOD FOR ME.

IF YOU DON'T MIND ME SAYING, JESSE: FOR A MAN WHO'S LOST HIS FAITH, YOU SEEM TO BE GETTING BY OKAY, Y'KNOW?

I'M CONSUMED BY INNER TURMOIL--

urrrrrp

HE'S GOT IT, TOO.

...DUNNO FOR SURE. WHAT I BELIEVE AN' DON'T BELIEVE'S BEEN CHANGIN' BY THE SECOND EVER SINCE THIS THING STARTED...

YOU'RE LOOKIN' FOR GOD--I MEAN LITERALLY, NOT SOME SOUL-SEARCHIN' BULLSHIT--WHERE THE HELL'RE YOU SUPPOSED TO START? JERUSALEM? ROME? TOP OF A MOUNTAIN? BILLY GRAHAM?

FIGURE A BLIND MAN IN GREENWICH VILLAGE IS AS LIKELY AS ANYTHING, HUH?

H--

YOU OKAY THERE? I'LL TRY NOT TO WAKE YOU IN THE MORNING.

AYE, JUST DON'T FLING WIDE YER CURTAINS TO FLOOD THE ROOM WITH GLORIOUS SUNLIGHT. YOU'LL GET A BIG SURPRISE, I'M TELLIN' YOU.

I LIKE THOSE TWO A LOT. I MEAN, I KNOW THERE'S A WHOLE LOT YOU'RE NOT TELLING ME ABOUT THEM--

AYE, THEY'RE A GOOD LAUGH FOR A PAIR OF IRAQI AGENTS.

G'NIGHT, SI.

G'NIGHT, BILLY-JOE-JIM-BOB.

167

YOU BEEN TALKING TO A GUY CALLED COLTRANE, TOOL? SI COLTRANE?

uh, NO, LIEUTENANT. NOT THAT I KNOW OF.

NOT THAT YOU KNOW OF.

HE'S A REPORTER. NAME'S ON THIS ARTICLE IN NEWS-WEEK RIGHT HERE. HE SEEMS TO KNOW YOU, BRIDGES AND YOUR LATEST CASE INSIDE-OUT. *NOW WHAT HAVE I TOLD YOU ABOUT TALK-ING TO THE PRESS?*

LT. ET...

WORLD'S GREATE MOM

BUT I--

HE'S GOT THE CONROY KILLING IN HERE, TOOL! WE RELEASED IT FOUR O'CLOCK YESTERDAY, TOO LATE FOR THEM GOING TO PRESS *BUT HE'S GOT IT IN!*

I--I--NO, WAIT, COLTRANE-- I THINK MAY-BE HE DID TRY TO ASK US SOME QUESTIONS BUT WE WOULDN'T HAVE SAID A *WORD,* I SWEAR! HE'S GOT TO HAVE FOLLOWED US--

IF BRIDGES HAD MET HIM EVEN BRIEFLY HE'D'VE NOTICED THE SON OF A BITCH TRAILING YOU A MILE OFF. *YOU* MISSING HIM I COULD BELIEVE, BUT NOT BRIDGES.

WHO, I CAN'T HELP BUT NOTICE, ISN'T HERE...

HE CALLED IN SICK, MA'AM. HE'S BEEN, WELL, ACTING KIND OF TWITCHY JUST LATELY. NOT REALLY HIMSELF.

I GUESS HE MIGHT'VE MISSED THIS REPORTER CHARACTER, FEELING LIKE THAT.

THAT'S SWELL.

WOR GRE

WORLD'S GREATEST MOM

GET OUT, TOOL.

168

I CAN'T REALLY BLAME HER. THIS IS THE HIGHEST-PROFILE SERIES OF HOMICIDES EVER FACED BY THIS PRECINCT, AND THE TWO OFFICERS SHE ASSIGNS CAN'T EVEN EXERCISE AN OUNCE OF DISCRETION...

SO I'VE GOT NO LEADS, NO SUSPECT, NO PARTNER--AND BRIDGES HAS BEEN ACTING WEIRD; I COULD SWEAR HE WAS CRYING WHEN HE GOT OUT'VE THE CAR LAST NIGHT--

CALL FOR YOU, TOOL.

AND NO LUCK.

TOOL.

GOOD MORNING, DETECTIVE.

YES, IT'S ME AGAIN.

I'M SORRY TO NOTE THAT DETECTIVE BRIDGES IS ILL TODAY, BUT ON THE OTHER HAND HE WON'T BE THERE TO DETRACT FROM YOUR MOMENT OF GLORY...

HOW ON EARTH DID HE KNOW ABOUT BRIDGES--?

VENUCCI! FOR CRYING OUT LOUD!

OKAY, OKAY! JESUS!

I'VE COME TO A DECISION ABOUT WHAT I'VE BEEN DOING, AND I WANTED YOU TO BE THE FIRST TO KNOW. I'M AT THE GROUND FLOOR APARTMENT OF THREE-HUNDRED-FIFTEEN WEST FORTY-FIFTH STREET...

AND DETECTIVE?

YES?

I'VE GOT A LOT TO SAY FOR MYSELF.

BRING A BIG S.W.A.T. TEAM.

I THINK I'M GONNA PUKE...

WOULDN'T MAKE A WHOLE LOT'VE DIFFERENCE TO THIS THING. WANT ME TO PULL OVER?

NO, I...I'LL BE OKAY. I JUST DIDN'T REALIZE I DRANK SO MUCH LAST NIGHT.

SHOULDA STAYED IN BED AN' SLEPT IT OFF.

I THOUGHT THE FRESH AIR WOULD BE GOOD FOR ME.

NOT IN MANHATTAN. ONLY FRESH AIR WE GET IN THIS TOWN IS WHEN SOMEBODY CUTS A FART.

THIS IS IT...

OKAY, JESSE: THIS GUY ISN'T TOO FOND OF ME, LIKE I TOLD YOU. YOU WALK AROUND TO THE FRONT OF THE BUILDING ON THE RIGHT, GO IN, UP THE STAIRS AND IT'S THE APARTMENT ON THE TOP FLOOR.

AN' I'M LOOKIN' FOR THE BIG MAN...

THE BIG MAN.

COMING?

uh-uh, I'LL WAIT WITH SI. I THINK I NEED TO SIT STILL FOR A WHILE.

170

I SEE HIM EVERY FEW YEARS-- WHENEVER HE'S IN TOWN, YOU KNOW. HE MOVES AROUND A HELL OF A LOT. GOT A GIRLFRIEND IN SAN FRANCISCO I THINK.

CASSIDY HAS A *GIRLFRIEND*?

HARD AS IT MAY BE TO BELIEVE. I MEAN, HE'S GOTTA HAVE GIRLS ALL OVER THE PLACE, BUT SHE'S THE ONLY ONE HE EVER MENTIONED.

I THOUGHT, WELL, HIM BEING THE WAY HE IS--

--HIS ONLY INTEREST IN WOMEN WAS DIETARY, YEAH. I THOUGHT SO TOO, AT FIRST.

I DON'T THINK CASS'S, *uh*, CONDITION HAS MUCH EFFECT ON HIS OVERALL LIFESTYLE. HE HAS THE SAME URGES MOST OF US DO--IT'S JUST HE'S MORE INCLINED TO INDULGE THEM.

THE ONLY REAL DIFFERENCE IS, THE REST OF US DON'T *BLOW UP* WHEN WE GO OUT IN THE SUN...

WE DON'T DRINK PEOPLE'S BLOOD, EITHER.

TRUE, TRUE...

FUCK, I DUNNO. I'M NOT SAYIN' HE'S A SAINT, BUT I NEVER SAW HIM DO THAT TO ANYONE WHO WASN'T GONNA DIE ANYWAY. OR DIDN'T DESERVE TO GET IT ONE WAY OR ANOTHER.

HOW YOU FEELING NOW, BY THE WAY?

OKAY, I GUESS. THIRSTY.

YOU KNOW WHAT, I THINK I GOT A SNAPPLE IN HERE SOMEWHERE. CHECK THE GLOVE COMPARTMENT, I'LL SEE IF IT'S IN BACK...

DON'T SEE IT. ANY LUCK?

173

178

I'M SORRY, TULIP. THIS MUST HAVE BEEN A TERRIBLE SHOCK FOR YOU.

AND THERE'S WORSE TO COME, I'M AFRAID.

YOU REMEMBER THE SERIAL KILLER STORY I'M COVERING? WELL, NOT TO PUT TOO FINE A POINT ON IT: I'M HIM.

EASIEST EXCLUSIVES I EVER GOT, BELIEVE ME.

AS WELL AS THAT, THERE IS NO "BIG MAN." THAT WAS ALL JUST BULLSHIT I MADE UP.

YOUR BOYFRIEND'S WALKING INTO THE HOME OF ONE *DETECTIVE PAULIE BRIDGES,* WHO-- YOU MIGHT REMEMBER-- IS SUPPOSED TO BE ON THE TRAIL OF THE KILLER.

WHY HAVE I DONE THIS? WELL, THE FIRST THING I FOUND WHILE HACKING THROUGH VARIOUS DATABASES--LOOKING FOR THE RELIGIOUS PHENOMENA JESSE WANTED--WAS AN *A.P.B.* LISTED IN THE F.B.I. COMPUTER...

REVEREND JESSE CUSTER, MISSING SINCE A MYSTERIOUS EXPLOSION KILLED HIS CONGREGATION IN ANNVILLE, TEXAS. *AND* SUBSEQUENT CURIOUS GOINGS-ON RESULTED IN THE DEATHS OF SEVERAL DOZEN MORE CIVILIANS AND LAW OFFICERS.

WUH-- WUH--

SO I PUT TWO AND TWO TOGETHER, AND I GOT: REPORTER DELIVERS DANGEROUS FUGITIVE TO HERO COP. REPORTER THEN ABOVE SUSPICION IN ANY INVESTIGATION FOLLOWING DISCOVERY OF SEVERAL *BODIES* IN HIS APARTMENT.

DANGEROUS FUGITIVE'S GIRLFRIEND TOO *DEAD* TO SAY DIFFERENT.

179

SO THEY PULLED THE BAYONET OUT OF HIS NECK AND STUFFED HIM IN A BODYBAG, AND THEN THEY STARTED TAKING BETS ON WHETHER THE OTHER GUY WOULD MAKE IT.

THE APARTMENT TURNED OUT TO BELONG TO SI COLTRANE, THE REPORTER THAT WAS TAILING US ON THE CASE--SO I FIGURED PAULIE'D FIND IT PRETTY FUNNY THAT THE CREEP *WAS* THE CASE--

NO ANSWER FROM DETECTIVE BRIDGES.

NO ANSWER?

BUT HOW CAN THAT BE? HE CALLED IN SICK-- WHY ISN'T HE HOME?

AND THAT'S WHEN IT HIT ME.

IF COLTRANE WAS TAILING US, HE KNEW WHERE WE BOTH LIVED--

AND IF PAULIE WAS HOME BUT HE COULDN'T PICK UP THE PHONE--

GET UNITS TO--

AND THAT'S HOW I RAN THE INTERSECTION--

AND THAT'S WHY THE UNLUCKIEST COP IN THE WORLD HAD TO HANDLE THIS ONE BY HIMSELF.

NOW WHO THE FUCK ARE YOU?!

HHHH--!

PAULIE, WE HAVE TO BE GOING--

SIT THE FUCK DOWN!

YOU AIN'T GOING ANYWHERE! THIS MOTHERFUCKER'S SEEN ENOUGH TO RUIN ME!

NO KIDDING.

AFTERNOON, DETECTIVE BRIDGES. JESSE.

BOYS.

HEY, YOU READ THIS TOO? ISN'T IT GREAT?

JESUS! YOU'RE THAT REPORTER!

LISTEN, I KNOW THIS LOOKS WEIRD--

LOOK, WHAT ARE YOU DOING HERE?

I'M DOING MY CIVIC DUTY, DETECTIVE. I'M HELPING YOU TO APPREHEND...

A VERY DANGEROUS CRIMINAL.

188

WE REALLY *DO* HAVE TO GO NOW, PAULIE...

AND, *uh,* IF YOU'RE THROWING ANOTHER OF THESE LITTLE PARTIES -- DON'T CALL US, OKAY?

PAULIE, *uh...* CORRECT ME IF I'M WRONG, BUT ...DON'T YOU HATE GAY PEOPLE?

I DO, JOHNNY, I DO, I DO!

BUT FUCK, I WAS JUST -- I MEAN, WE'RE OUT THERE ON THE STREETS TAKING DOWN ALL THE FUCKOS AND SCUM-BAGS *AND I HATE THEM SO MUCH,* AND SUDDENLY IT WASN'T ENOUGH TO BE *TOUGH,* OR *MACHO* -- I WANTED TO BE EVEN MORE --

SO I TRIED TO TAKE IT OUT ON THE *SCUM* BUT I REALIZED WHAT I WANTED WAS TO *TAKE* PAIN, NOT JUST HAND IT OUT...AND... ONE NIGHT, I SAW THOSE THREE GUYS AND I WANTED --

OH JESUS, JOHNNY!

I THINK I'M GAY!

ARE YOU SURE YOU'RE NOT JUST FUCKED IN THE HEAD?

THAT WAS THE FIRST TIME IN MY LIFE I USED PROFANITY.

BUT IT'S NOT EASY, BEING A COP.

BLARNEY STONE

BASTARD!!

MUNNGH

...SHITE. DIDN'T MEAN TO DO THAT.

OUGHTA LEAVE, HUH?

OUGHTA LEAVE. SORRY ABOUT THAT, JIMMY.

IT JUST FUCKIN' PISSES ME OFF, THAT'S ALL.

I GUESS A FELLA TRYIN' TO GET YOU KILLED'LL DO THAT.

I MEAN, YOU THINK YOU'VE GOT A GOOD FRIEND, RIGHT? SOME- ONE YOU CAN RELY ON, THEY'RE ALWAYS GONNA BE THERE FOR YOU...

AN' THEY GET RIGHT IN *HERE*, BUT THAT'S ALL RIGHT BECAUSE YOU THINK YOU'VE GOT THEM THE SAME WAY...

AN' THEN IT TURNS OUT THEY'RE JUST ANOTHER *FUCKER*.

THINK I KNOW THAT FEELIN'.

SHIT, AYE, I SUPPOSE YOU DO. MORE'N ANYONE.

WHAT THE HELL, CASS.

CAN'T ALL BE FUCKERS, CAN THEY?

FOR SINGLE-HANDEDLY TAKING DOWN MASS MURDERER SIMON "SERIAL SI" COLTRANE, JOHN TOOL MADE SERGEANT A MONTH LATER, AND LIEUTENANT THE FOLLOWING YEAR.

COP STOPS KILLER SOLO

DETECTIVE JOHN TOOL NYPD HERO

THE YEAR AFTER THAT HE LOST BOTH ARMS IN A HORRIFIC GLAZING ACCIDENT.

PAUL BRIDGES LEFT THE FORCE, BUT MADE A POINT OF KEEPING IN TOUCH WITH HIS FORMER PARTNER...

WHO IS THIS?

CASSIDY WENT WEST, BUT NOT BEFORE STOPPING FOR A SNACK IN HIS FAVORITE BROOKLYN NEIGHBORHOOD--

WHO YOU CALLIN' GUINEA, YOU MOTHER-FUCKIN' MICK?

OF THE REVEREND JESSE CUSTER AND MS. TULIP O'HARE, THERE HAS SO FAR BEEN NO NEWS.

Look for these other Vertigo books:
All Vertigo titles are Suggested for Mature Readers

To find more collected editions and monthly comic books from DC Comics,
call 1-888-COMIC BOOK for the nearest comics shop or go to your local book store.

Visit us at www.dccomics.com